African Magic Series

BLOOD MAGIC

MONIQUE JOINER SIEDLAK

Oshun Publications

ISBN: 978-1-950378-59-3

Cover Design by MJS

Cover Image by phakimata@depositphotos.com

Published by Oshun Publications

www.oshunpublications.com

Other Books in the Series

African Spirituality Beliefs and Practices

Hoodoo
Seven African Powers: The Orishas
Cooking for the Orishas
Lucumi: The Ways of Santeria
Voodoo of Louisiana
Haitian Vodou
Orishas of Trinidad
Connecting With Your Ancestors

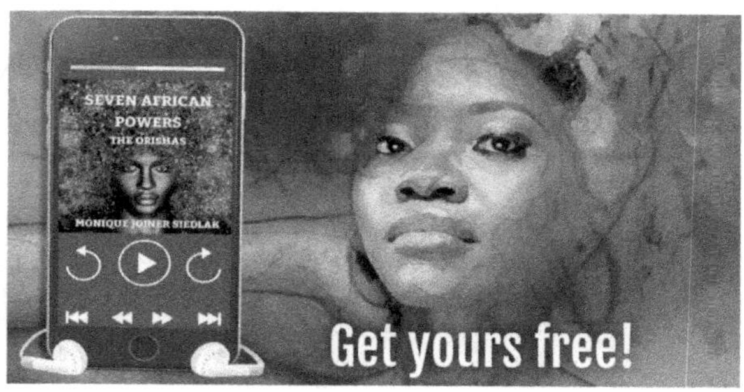

Want to learn about African Magic, Wicca, or even Reiki while cleaning your home, exercising, or driving to work? I know it's tough these days to simply find the time to relax and curl up with a good book. This is why I'm delighted to share that I have books available in audiobook format.

Best of all, you can get the audiobook version of this book or any other book by me for free as part of a 30-day Audible trial.

Members get free audiobooks every month and exclusive discounts. It's an excellent way to explore and determine if audiobook learning works for you.

If you're not satisfied, you can cancel anytime within the trial period. You won't be charged, and you can still keep your book. To choose your free audiobook, visit:

www.mojosiedlak.com/free-audiobooks

WANT UPDATES,
FREEBIES & GIVEAWAYS?!
MONIQUE JOINER SIEDLAK
THE
ORISHAS
JOIN MY
NEWSLETTER!
mojosiedlak.com/newsletter-signup

Contents

Introduction

Blood magic, you guessed it, is performing magic with blood as the primary factor. It involves casting the most powerful kind of spells. Blood magic is an old tradition whose history firmly predates creation.

Using blood in a ritual or spell is about much more than a witch just cutting themselves. The origin of the blood is one of the most significant elements.

Blood use is equivalent to every facet of witchcraft because of its tremendous power. Blood sustains us all. Without blood, survival would never be conceivable. Apart from providing us life through nourishment, blood connects people from a spiritual and sacred means. It draws on the donor's nature and personality, acting as a mystical fount for the magic that follows, preparing it, and giving it purpose. That's what makes it such a potent factor.

Where the body has is cut is likewise significant, and how the witch stores and uses the blood has profound symbolic significance. They frequently refer to these three items as the origin, the cut, and the process.

When practicing blood magic spells, treat blood with absolute respect while handling it with care. Keeping the blood pure and free of sickness is what'll make the blood magic spells effectively. Blood serves as the spirit of a person. Therefore, it can manipulate their energy when added to spell casting. You can use your blood or that of someone else depends on the structure of your spell. For the latter, you'll be required to get a clean sample of the subject's blood before beginning with your spell casting. Blood magic spells are among the most potent spells in witchcraft. Meaning that if you can accurately cast a spell, your chances of obtaining whatever you wish will be very high. Make sure you've worked the spell over and over so that your chances of messing up are between zero to nothing. If you are a beginner, requesting advice from an accomplished witch or spell caster is very much suggested.

Blood magic is more straightforward than more complex practices. Whether it looks like a vulnerability of the belief or strength depends on a witch's attitude to magic.

As with all magical customs, witches do not have to use blood magic if they don't want to. Blood magic is a metaphysical framework that witches can adopt to add significance to their rituals. It is not on a standard list of components that will make a ritual fail if they do not add them.

ONE

Why Use Blood in Magic?

Blood Magic, also recognized as Blood Sorcery, is an ancient and severe kind of magic. This mystical but forbidden magic is used to cast spells and charms. Curses created with blood, the very bodily fluid, which is the influential strength and the essence of life in the working of magic, are potent. It may be a representation of a sacrifice. Still, it may also be the loss of life that sustains the spell. Blood magic is also generally practiced in Blood Rituals.

Some blood may be made to be more potent than others. Common types are human blood, the caster's own blood, the blood of royalty, an extraordinary family lineage, a youth's blood, or a virgin's blood. Sometimes simply a particular individual's blood has power, and any other blood is ineffective.

Every participant has the natural strength within their blood to feed the magic. This is an ancestral perspective that predates word-based magic and is thought by some to be more powerful. Blood Magic is sorcery based on blood usage, a significant ingredient in many rituals, spells, and other supernatural nature situations.

The first point you need to understand about blood magic is that it's not naturally evil. Some people incorrectly assume that using blood in magic is 'mysterious' or somehow only linked with malicious intentions. This is honestly not true.

The negative undertones begin back to that fear of blood. Fear of our own mortality, fear of authority, etc., are the kind of driving factors behind a fear of blood. Indeed, if you are afraid of blood, you might prefer to bypass blood altogether. It's not for everybody.

But blood is like any item you would need in magic. It's a potent tool, but a tool nonetheless. It's neither compassionate nor malicious in its own right. You could use it for whatever goals. Like any other object or tool, it's not advised to use it for unethical purposes.

Blood magic works because of the link between an individual's living blood and their fundamental nature. While conjurers argue over the specific nature of this relation, whether or not it expresses a person's spirit or something less metaphysical, what is undeniable is that the blood carries a mystical tie to a person's fundamental elements. When blood is spilled, it is conceivable to produce the magic that takes on that individual's essential aspects and form mystical bonds with them.

Practitioners of blood magic teach fundamental aspects that impact an individual are also present in some way in their blood, as are their connections to one another. The lovers' blood is notoriously potent. Blood occultists believe that the strength of their desire for one another is contained or echoed in the blood, as is the bond between parent to child and brother to sister. Of particular concern in the last example is that blood magic teaches that the bond's strength between family members is echoed in the blood even when a sibling or child is adopted. This link between a person and their blood works both ways - the magician can use the blood to fuel the power of their magic with the owner's essential qualities. But they can still use the blood to produce links and bonds to that individual.

TWO

Blood Magic Is Not Blood Sacrifice

THERE ARE STILL RELIGIONS AND TRADITIONS THAT USE BLOOD and draw all the community support in places like Santeria, Palo Mayombe, or Voodoo. It is regrettable to learn modern Western occultists attack practitioners of religions that consist of sacrifice. There is no problem with being against the practice. Still, we shouldn't criticize others based on an inadequate perception. That is to say, you can't argue someone is sacrificing an animal to produce injury and terror when all they are actually doing is making a meal. Unless you are vegan yourself, you can't criticize the use of animals for food, either for people or for spirits.

Human blood is never given in Haitian Vodou, despite stereotypes to the contrary. Blood can be given in the rituals around making animal offerings. In this way, the animal practically always becomes food for ritual members once the spirits have accepted their share. It is possible to regard sacrifice in the belief of other offerings of considerable worth given to the spirits. An entire Vodou society will commit to initiation ceremonies or annual celebrations of a particular ritual, such as the extreme amount of effort, wealth, resources, and time. However, Haitian Vodou does not set these offerings as being more precious or greater than the absolute sacrifice of an animal's life to give protection, blessing, and nourishment for that society and its members.

With Haitian Vodou, animals are raised primarily for the purpose of food and for ritual-connected food or ritual objectives where the animal cannot be feasted upon at a later time. These animals are bred by the community that will sacrifice them. Before they are offered, they are washed up, dressed up, and prepared by the community. They will be brought into the Vodou temple, known as a peristyle, and presented with several different foods. One of these foods is determined ahead of time as being the official sacrificing food. The animal is told what will take place. If it is prepared to be sacrificed, it will eat the sanctioned food to represent this. Only if the animal eats the specific food will it be offered to the spirits for the sacrifice. If the animal eats anything else first, it must be let loose because it is reluctant to do the work.

The sacrifice usually is confused with blood offerings. Blood sacrifice actually doesn't have a place in a current Neopagan context. Yet, there are organized practices that still perform blood sacrifices. In a present Druid context, gifts are generally any tangible item used to present to the gods. There are examples where Neopagans will sacrifice some of their own blood as a form of a blood oath in rare occurrences. The slaying of a live animal is another form of ancient sacrifice or offering that really is not something that is all that common in a Neopagan context. Most of us buy our meat already slaughtered for consumption. Still, there are alternatives to give a portion of that meat as a sacrifice in the form of the shared feast.

Presenting offerings to the gods cannot possibly be a bad thing. Like prayer and interaction with one's spiritual community, sometimes it's something you can never get enough of. Giving notable contributions that take effort, non-blood sacrifices are just more of the same. Pagans do not need to provide blood sacrifice. Unless they realize the background of that act, have experienced people who can implement it for them, and have a specific need to do it. Either they need to share ritual meals in a place where they need to slaughter their own meat. They prefer to bless that action by giving their food animals to the gods, or their gods require it of them, and no alternative choices are adequate.

Depending on the situation and the structure, the sacrifice can strengthen connections by being a blessing for assistance or guidance that has been given. It can be carried out as an agreement for future action; it can be extended as a replacement for someone else's life. Sacrifice can symbolize a full offering of self to the gods, goddesses, or spirits. Or it can be a consideration for a foreseen mutual benefit. There is no customary understanding that pertains to all sacrifices from all individuals to all spirits or gods. Like its essence as a different and extraordinary thing, each one has a particular and unique purpose.

Sacrifice is as much about establishing communications with the spirits, gods, goddesses, and among members of a spiritual community. It is an action of bountifulness. When we open sacred space, we invite the ancestries into the ritual as family and kin. That association is developed on sharing and trust. We sacrifice to strengthen our relationships and make them stronger. Gods give their blessings through sacrifice and increase their connection.

THREE

Blood Magic Is Not Evil

Blood magic isn't fundamentally evil; it is just how the spell caster decides to employ blood magic. You can choose to use it for positive spells, such as for protection or healing spells. Or you can decide to use it for malicious intent, forcing someone to care for you, harming someone, or an act of vengeance. Mainstream media has given blood magic a lousy title. Television often characterizes evil witches using blood magic to injure others and cause someone to love them and do everything they demand. While blood magic can be performed in this fashion, most people do not use it like this. It is up to you to determine how to work blood magic but recognize that everything includes consequences, so be ready to assume any results from good magic and the bad.

An excellent implement to have for blood magic is the lancets diabetics use to check their blood sugar.

Thanks to Hollywood, the populace has developed to identify witchcraft with ritualistic sacrifices of humans and animals, which is nothing but lies. Just because blood is the primary element in blood magic spells doesn't mean you'll have to kill anybody. Just a slight drop of blood, either from you or the target of your spell, is sufficient for your spell casting rituals. It is likewise important to mention that most individuals who practice blood magic spell always do it for good. For example, if you wish your husband to love you more, you can invariably offer him some red wine mixed with a drop of your fresh menstrual blood. This ensures that both of you are happier in your marriage since he'll find you much more attractive. A few individuals might perform blood magic spells for hostile reasons. But in most instances, all they want to do is punish someone who did them wrong. Therefore, the first rule beginners need to grasp and observe is that blood magic spells don't involve killing for blood. Once that has been recognized, then they can continue to understand what blood magic spells and witchcraft as a whole discipline is all about.

FOUR

Blood Magic Rituals

Blood magic rituals are potent and have more significant effects compared to other kinds of spells. Beginners should be cautious when using blood magic. The added power that spells have when performed with blood is critical to understand this kind of magic before applying it. This type of magic is presently conducted by those who practice Santeria.

In addition to Africa, Haiti, and the United States, it's more so in the poorer countries. Since hunting is a way to survive, they perform blood rituals with animals. Following using the animal's blood for their ceremony, they will share and consume it with everybody in their village. Blood magic is another medium to apply in rituals that can help you reach and realize precisely what you want. Empowering you to fulfill your desires further. It adds a huge deal of energy to your spell rituals, an energy that you cannot negate. It can help you conquer an illness or shield you from severe accidents and assist you in other significant events.

Blood is a potent tool that many cannot even stand to use because blood makes them uncomfortable. Those who can mentally handle using their blood can significantly strengthen their spells' capacity, even as novices. Humans are made up of blood. It's blood that keeps us alive. Blood gives us strength. It travels faster when our heart rate goes up. Women bleed once a month during their period and likewise when delivering babies. Blood gives us life.

On the other hand, too much blood, leaving us, can lead to death. Blood has so much strength within our bodies that it keeps us alive, so it is purely logical to create more potent spells with blood magic. When we use blood in our magic, we are putting a part of ourselves into the spell, giving the spell even more life.

A blood ritual is any ritual that requires the voluntary surrender of blood. A typical blood ritual is the blood brother ritual, which began in ancient Europe and Asia. Two or more individuals, often male, commingle their blood. This symbolically brings the members together into one family. This can be a hazardous practice where blood-borne infections are involved. The method of safe, sterilized equipment such as a lancet can reduce this dilemma.

Body piercing can likewise be part of a blood ritual. Though piercing does not consistently cause bleeding, it indeed can. Piercing has been used in several indigenous societies throughout the world, commonly as a symbolic celebration of transition, a symbolic death, and revival, an induction, or for reasons of magical protection.

Blood rituals generally involve a symbolic death and rebirth, as actual bodily birth requires bleeding. Blood is frequently identified as highly powerful and continually as unclean. Blood sacrifice is commonly viewed by the practitioners of invocation, ritual magic, and spell casting to increase such actions' energy. The Native American Sun Dance is customarily followed by a blood sacrifice.

Many blood rituals require two or more parties cutting themselves or each other, followed by blood consumption. The members may see the surrender or take in the blood to generate energy use as a healing, erotic, or mental stimulus. In other instances, blood is an essential factor as the sacrifice or ingredient for a spell. Blood rituals are practiced by several groups of people, including those having political affiliations or religious. Some of the ways involving blood have been practiced for many centuries and are still being practiced even now.

FIVE

When and When Not to Use Blood Magic

BELIEVE IT OR NOT, YOU CAN UTILIZE BLOOD IN YOUR MAGIC IN just about every spell and spell working. Whether it's dressing candles, blending to potions, using on petition papers, etc., on the condition that it doesn't expressly exclude blood magic. You need to determine the best way to incorporate blood into the spell for each spell you choose to transform to blood magic.

Using Blood Magic

Is the spell going to contain physical ingredients that remain after the spell is cast? Is it mainly ceremonial and energy endeavor? Once the spell is cast, will any physical items be representing the spell? You can effortlessly add blood in or on the spell object, depending on what's suitable.

You can also incorporate your blood work into the spell casting itself, adequately dispose of the ingredients, and clean the space soon after. This can mean putting in a few drops of blood onto a candle, in a glass, or on a bit of paper with inscriptions, symbols, sigils, etc., that you would destroy during the spell casting.

If you are doing a curse and want to include your own blood, you would not merely add it to the complete spell for the most part. The best approach would be to use your blood on or with the objects intended to put the curse in motion or produce harm from the curse.

Ensure that you focus on your intent while you are making use of the blood to really get the boost to connect. For the most part, you would add blood first when doing blood spells.

When and where blood magic is precisely your best choice, I can't tell you. Still, you should use it solely in the absolute need for the most severe factors.

At what point should you use blood magic for protection. You would want it as protection from something significant. Not for something minor. Suppose your neighbor is a nuisance, regularly allow trash in their yard to blow into yours. In that case, you're not going to use blood magic to hinder them. You're not planning to move, are you? You can be diplomatic by speaking with them. It may be they don't notice it, and once it's pointed out, you may see less blowing on your side of the property line.

A substantial blood magic protection would be when there is a potential for life-changing severe threats such as a crime or accident.

Using blood magic for your health and well-being is perfect, but not small matters like small burns, sore throats, sprains, cuts, bruises, etc. This would be for severe health issues like illness, injuries, surgery, or breaking unhealthy habits.

Having an urgent need, such as if you were on the brink of being destitute or starving, you could use blood magic to bring what you need to live. It's not for frivolous items like cash for a brand new car, while the one you're driving works fine. Yes, it's ugly as all get out, but it does its job.

What Blood is the Wrong Blood

You have to remember, blood magic is powerful and should not be taken lightly. Even though it's been said before, it should be mentioned once again.

Cutting yourself is not necessary. Using more blood is not going to make your spell work faster or better. A little does go a long way.

For women, you would never use menstrual blood in the same manner that you would use a drop of blood from your finger. The menstruation blood is strictly for love spells. Drawing things towards you. It is not to be used for hexing or cursing someone.

If you are using the blood of animals, do not use the blood of road kill. The fact it is road kill is enough for you not to use it.

Never practice blood magic unless you're fully willing to receive whatever the repercussions may be, which means considering them through very deliberately.

Not under any condition use it to target other people without their consent except, of course, it's dangerous required for protection. I had no issue evicting a terrifying family member who refused to leave my home and jeopardized my children's life with a gun.

At no time, use it in love or relationship magic. I've always said bonds between people need to be naturally developed, not forced. Blood magic can transform a likely bond into a chain. In other words, emotional captivity. Knowing someone is with you because you made them is not happiness.

SIX

Practicing Safe Blood Magic

Blood magic is not about hurting or maiming yourself. You don't need to take blood from a major artery or vein. Really, I've said it before, a little does go a long way.

Treat all blood like it is infected. Especially if it's not your own.

Many diseases are able to survive in the blood even after it leaves the body. This is something where you cannot accept someone's word for. So if you are handling someone else's blood, always wear gloves.

Lastly, always get rid of lancets, needles, pins, soiled alcohol pads, etc., safely. Do not just drop it in the trash bin and think nothing of it. Remember, all our instruments need to be given respect, and anything with blood on it should be deposed of correctly.

Collecting Blood

The collection of blood takes place in many different forms. For blood magic, one approach is to fingerpick.

Fingerpick involves drawing a tiny amount of blood from the end of a finger. It is over immediately and includes surprisingly little in the way of preparation. It's always fresh since you only need a few drops for your spell or ritual.

The best approach is to use a sterile lancet. Select an area on the surface of the palm-side of the second or third finger. Sanitize the pre prick area by using a sanitizing gel.

Sanitize a small pricking instrument, such as a pin or lancet. keep the finger in an upward position and prick or lance the finger. Press firmly on your finger when making the pinprick. Doing so will help you to attain the quantity of blood you need.

Moderate pressure may be applied just below the puncture site to obtain a second drop of blood. Avoid squeezing the finger. If needed, lightly massage from the hand to near the puncture site to get the required blood amount.

Clean the wound promptly and put some antibiotic ointment on it. If you notice it's still bleeding, placed gauze or a bandage on it. Anything that has been touched with blood should be disposed of at the end of your spell or ritual.

Disinfect surfaces of your workspace, tools, and any other instruments after performing blood magic.

Most importantly, keep the wound clean as it heals.

SEVEN

Using Menstrual Blood

MENSTRUAL BLOOD CARRIES A LENGTHY PAST OF BEING dreaded by men. They have been offered drugs against identifying with, touching, or engaging sex with menstruating women, for their blood carries the power to harm. Ancient Romans thought the menstruating woman's influence could blunt swords, blast fruit, sour wine, rust iron, and cloud mirrors. The Talmud advises that husband and wife are sexually separated during menstruation and for a week afterward to assure cleanness.

In Christianity, menstrual blood was thought to produce demons and to desecrate shrines. Menstruating women were prevented from participating in communion up to the late 17th century. In some cases, they weren't even allowed to step into the church.

At the sheer utterance of all things monthly period, men and women cringe and flee for cover. Thanks to social media transformation, many have been informed and communicative about issues connected with menstrual well-being. Even though we aren't near where we have to be, it has not been continuously like this.

In ancient ages, women were singled out and generally

described as evil at that time of the month. Some were not allowed near their family, while others were subjugated to bleeding shelters where they were kept for the 2 to 6 days they would bleed. It was presumed they would threaten their lives because of the evil on their heads.

While some were not so positive, mainly out of pure ignorance of the whole situation, others accepted the natural circumstance and even found benefits.

Ancient Egyptians thought that a first menstrual flow meant that the adolescent was becoming attuned to the Great Goddess. They incorporated menstrual blood into their medicinal and beauty regime. It was thought that menstrual blood reduced the appearance of stretch marks. It was also applied as a tightening and firming formula to improve sagging breasts and thighs and used in remedies and ointments to treat various conditions.

In ancient times witches and Priestesses respected menstrual blood. They created and drank liquids incorporating their menstrual blood to magnify their magical powers. An elixir known as the drink of immortality, they also combined the blood with semen for warriors. They were invincible on the field of battle.

The most routine and moderately unexpected use of this sacred blood is ceremonies and rituals in the Hoodoo custom. A native African-American folk spirituality Hoodoo is recognized to have been originated from several spiritual actions, practices, and faiths in West Africa, particularly Nigeria, Congo, Togo, and Benin. Also known as conjure, root work, root doctoring, laying tricks, working the root, and more, Hoodoo is practiced by native African-Americans. as mentioned earlier, they are descendants of slaves sold from the countries during the Trans-Atlantic slave trade.

Hoodoo is represented by rituals and potions containing bodily excretions and fluids like menstrual blood, seminal fluid, saliva, sweat, and urine.

Some maintain it is just pheromone or scent magic. Characterized as pheromones' aspect to bring about the interest between two people. Powerful enough to transform desires. Others have criticized this statement and find it absolutely ludicrous to add body mixes to food and drink. That does not bring to a stop hoodoo women from engaging in and working conforming to their beliefs. There has been an enormous display of reports women have affirmed by this action generating satisfying outcomes.

Women would often incorporate the blood from their monthly flow with their lovers' drink, which they thought is an unquestionable means to seize his aroused awareness. The concept behind this is that the woman's odor or aroma will be sealed into the object of her affections sphere of attention. After drinking this mixture several times, the unaware male or female falls unavoidably in love with the person who made the concoction. Their spirits are joined for all time. There are substitute recipes that use urine and sweat for these rituals or a mix of fluids.

In some cases, the males are aware of this ingredient in their drinks and their outcomes. They look at it as a blood agreement. And have granted to them and also as a form to bond with their significant ones.

It is crucial to indicate that practices of this sort are not to be made light of as they may have disastrous ethical, legal, and spiritual repercussions.

Collecting Menstrual Blood

Menstrual blood can be a handy ingredient in various potions and other spells. A menstrual or diva cup is used to collect your menstrual blood. Once you collected the blood, be sure you take a label on the vial and the type of blood it is, and when you collected it. To maintain freshness, keep in the refrigerator. It will last longer.

If you're looking to use dried blood in a powder, then spread the blood out. Giving the blood more contact with the air will allow it to dry fast. Once dried, you can scrape the blood and grind it into a powder. Label and date your container. Store in a dark, cool place.

Blood and Moon Magic

Using menstrual blood in spells and rituals while connecting to the moon is powerful. We have associated menstrual blood with the moon in many magical practices. For example, when working with Abuk or Mawu, using menstruating blood with spells, rituals, and the moon, you'll receive an extra boost.

Menstrual blood, which is associated with the phases of the Moon, is powerful. In mythologies, the Goddess's blood appears universally as mead, wise blood, wine, and milk. It is consumed as a magic charm for fertility, knowledge, healing, restoration, and immortality. Signified as an ambrosia drink, the blood of Isis bestowed divinity on pharaohs. According to ancient Taoism, red yin juice, which menstrual blood was called, was said to grant long life or immortality.

EIGHT

Alternatives to Blood

There are actually substitutes for using blood in blood magic spells.

As mentioned earlier, blood is the most influential factor for any magical workings. However, that doesn't alter the fact that many individuals can't get hold of blood. For example, some cannot stand the sight of blood, maybe a hemophiliac; possess a blood-borne disease, etc. Many beginners may not have the skill or instruments to carefully and safely draw blood for their blood magic rituals. Don't give up hope in practicing blood magic if any of this pertains to you.

Even though not quite as potent as blood, there are alternative items you can apply to tailor-make a spell and give it a jump. These items would be semen, any nail or hair clippings, urine, saliva, to provide an example. These taglocks are useful alternatives that will give strength to minor influence or workings when blood magic isn't applicable or recommended.

When you're first getting into magic, you should practice with these in the beginning before moving on to the blood. Give it some time. Analyze and work with these elements. You'll start to see an understanding of how much putting a part of yourself into a spell affects your magic.

If you wish to bind something to you, using some of your hair is just as effective. Hair is another potent personal object, and, similar to blood, it is related to connected items to your particular nature.

One more time, nothing is essentially good or evil. It all revolves around how you decide to use it. You will be okay with the understanding that you practice safe magic.

Animal Blood

Animal blood has comparable correspondences to human blood. It may be a suitable choice when you don't want to use your own blood. Similar to human blood, it is linked with both life and death. Traditionally, animal blood was a regular offering to the gods and goddesses in several cultures. Comparable to human blood, it provides an energy increase to spells and rituals.

Many will say not to use animal blood for blood magic spells. They feel practicing blood magic spells with blood from an unwilling subject will always have an undesired outcome. animals can't consent. However, consecrating the blood will make it more effective in your spell. Focus on the intent the blood will be used for.

Obtaining some animal blood may be tough, however you can find it if you look. You can ask your local butcher, even though there seem to be less and less of them if it would be possible to set some aside a bit of blood for you. Believe it or not, it's not a weird request for them. Animal blood is actually used to make Blodplättar (blood pancakes), Dinuguan (blood pudding stew), or my husband's favorite, Krupniok (blood sausage). So making this request is much more common than you think. You may also find congealed blood in any international grocery shops, which typically is pig's blood.

More Alternatives to Using Blood

If you are simply just not comfortable using blood, then don't. There are other substitutions to consider.

Blood and wine are corresponding symbols. If you want to give a religious offering to a spirit or deity, use red wine. Red wine has always been a standard spiritual sacrifice in the Catholic mass. It has even been used as a substitute for blood in many religious rituals.

Use pomegranate juice to show the indirect representation of the balance between life and death.

Known for their association with the Greek goddess Persephone and the Underworld, pomegranates have a strong fertility link. A symbol of Persephone, the pomegranate signifies the cycle of life and death.

You need to treat the substitute ingredients with ultimate reverence and care. This is because contamination will either make your spell less powerful or not powerful at all. It might help if you took the chance to understand how to deal with the blood substitutes, as pointed out earlier. You'll need to get to the point where you can carry out spells is second to nature, before carrying them out.

Blood magic is not scary, dark, or unsafe if approached with appropriate respect and caution. Because of its potency and rich symbolism, blood can be powerful additions to many spells.

NINE

What Blood Can Do

There are various ways you can use blood in magic, and none of it has to be unsafe. Examine working it in protection magic, healing spells, and even fertility magic. Incorporate it into your standard magical techniques. Some women prefer to use menstrual blood rather than pricking their fingers. If you choose to do this, use a menstrual cup to collect what you require for a spell.

Blood Offerings to Spirits

Giving your blood to call upon specific spirits to help with your magic can vastly expand the potency of your spells. You can provide a blood offering to many different spiritual individuals. Be sure to explore as much as possible before calling any one of them. Some of them may be extremely nasty and have ill-intent towards humans, even if you give them a blood offering.

Hoodoo Spirit Ritual Offering

There are hoodoo spirits that may be called upon to help you with magic spells, which may be more tempted to help if you use some blood when communicating with them. Make sure you do your research first before calling any of them. For example, Ogun is identified with blood and is reported that he can treat blood diseases. He loves blood, but it has been urged to only give him blood stored and not call on him if you are presently bleeding out of a cut or on your period.

Enhancing Spells

Blood can be to enhance spells. Whenever menstrual blood is in magic, spells seem to manifest quicker and more robust with less drive. You can write your intention or desire on a piece of paper, anoint the intention with menstrual blood, and later burn it.

Blood magic is an excellent addition for newcomers to practice in their spells when they require significant protection, such as when there could be something else substantial that could alter their life. This can include protection for your well-being. Use blood magic for healing severe injuries, combating sicknesses, or recuperating from surgeries. When employing this potent medium, you will be able to recognize a subtle distinction in your spells. Protection against something urgent, like needing your car repaired or you may lose your job, can call for using blood in your spells.

For a minor protection spell, blood magic really isn't necessary. Blood magic requires a large amount of energy. It can have significant ramifications, so use the spell is for something meaningful and worth any repercussions that may come.

Prosperity Spells

Remember, menstrual blood strengthens the outcome of your spell. This attribute makes menstrual blood well-suited with abundance spells and so on. An example would be writing down any money symbol. Whether it is a Dollar, Euro, Pound, or Zloty sign. Money bag, Fehu rune, etc., dab blood to it, then burn the paper and let the magic rise into the celestial atmosphere.

Folklore Blood Uses

There are so many practices for blood, according to folklore. Here are only a few you may have heard about:

Add nine drops of your menstrual blood to something your husband consumes, suitably his coffee, and he will never leave you.

If a woman is able to get a small amount of your blood on a piece of fabric, she can tie it up in a bag and carry it on her leg. The woman will drive you crazy in nine days.

If a woman needs her husband to stay away from other women, she can do so by placing a little of her blood in his coffee, and he will never leave her.

If you desire to keep your boyfriend or husband, take two drops of blood from your arm and add it to his coffee, and they will love you forever.

Let a woman write her boyfriend's name with a bit of her menstrual blood, and he will fall in love with her.

Prepare a vegetable soup like tomato soup and a few drops of your blood. It will cause a man to love you forever.

The red-hued waters of Kali's sacred well in India are reported to serve as the goddess's menstrual blood, and individuals make pilgrimages there to drink this precious water.

To cause someone to love you, draw the blood out of a live

pigeon, some of your blood, and write your suitor's name and your name with that blood on your arm or forehead, criss-crossing the names. He will always love you.

To control your lover's feet and make them come home each night, dab some of your blood inside each of their shoes.

TEN

Love Spells and Lust Spells

Magic users have been working menstrual blood in love spells and lust spells for forever. Menstrual blood helps you draw and command your objective. An example would be lighting a pink candle and writing on a piece of paper "(put in target's name) is my love." Visualize your desire being returned as you dab the note with menstrual blood. Later, burn the paper.

Spell to Bring Love to You

Everyone is searching for the perfect love spell. This love spell will bring the ideal individual with the perfect attributes you're looking for.

ITEMS NEEDED:

Two large Candles (one representing your future lover, one representing you)

Pink Ribbon

White Ribbon

A Pin

A List of Your Lover's Qualities
Six Drops of Your Blood
Anointing Oil

DIRECTIONS:

On Friday in the hour of Venus during a new moon, carve your full name and birthday into the candle whose color represents you. Consecrate candle as being you with anointing oil and three drops of your blood. Say:

"This candle represents me."

Put your candle on the right side of your altar.

Light your candle, visualizing yourself opening up to love.

With the candle representing the type of person you want in your life, carve that individual's qualities. As you carve each attribute, say:

"I invite in my life someone who is (traits you've listed)."

When you finished, consecrate with anointing oil and three drops of your blood, the candle signifying your lover. State:

"This candle signifies the person that I summon into my life to be my lover. I draw in my life a lover who has (state all traits)."

Place your prospective lover's candle on the left side of your altar, 14 inches apart from the candle symbolizing you.

Light your lover's candle. See them aware of your call.

Let the candles burn for 15 minutes. Extinguish the candles, recognizing that that person is on their way to you.

Every day, light the candles and move them each once inch closer to each other, realizing that you and that individual are now coming closer together.

Keep doing this until the candles meet. If you've encountered this person, tie the candles together with pink and white strings.

If you haven't met this individual and the candles have touched, continue lighting them, and visualize that you've met them. Sense how right it feels to have that individual in your world.

If the candles have finished by the time you haven't met them, don't give up. That individual may have moved closer to your location!

Repeat the spell through the next full moon cycle.

Love Root Spell

This spell will attract someone to you. It's your blood, which will cause it more potent.

ITEMS NEEDED:

Few Strands of Your Hair
Few Strands of Your Subject's Hair
2-3 Drops of Your Blood
Black Thread
Red Thread
Ceramic Dish
Soil
A Red Candle with Candle Holder
Piece Of St. John the Conqueror Root

DIRECTIONS:

Bind the root with the hair strands. Next, bind with the red and black thread. Be sure you use enough to secure the hair. Set root charm in the ceramic dish, covering it with soil.

Drop your blood onto the dirt. Light the candle and hold it over the dish. Let several big drops of red wax fall onto the soil over the root. Set the candle in a candle holder and let it continue burning.

After a week, the partner you desired will exhibit some genuine interest in you.

ELEVEN

Using Blood in Candle Magic

Candles are a fundamental component in any magical kit. They are used to strengthening and release energy. When using candles for magic, generally use a fresh candle for each spell. Candles will carry the vibration from the last use unless it's a spell or ritual going over several days.

The transformational energy of fire is channeled in candle magic. It is one of the oldest and most commonly practiced forms of magic. In doing candle magic, we are welcoming change into our lives. Fire is also a tool of illumination. When lighting a candle, we shed light on the world around us and, therefore, see our surroundings with much more clarity.

With candle magic, we can reconnect with the elements. This reconnection is vital for every living being, regardless of their beliefs. Witches, Christians, and Atheists are still people. Therefore, we all should be aware of the importance of the Earth and nature. How to tap into it for help when necessary. There is truly no limit to candle magic!

The reason candle magic works is by harnessing the energy of fire. In burning candles and opening up this energy, it can lead to an altered state of awareness, allowing the psyche and soul to open up to insight, positive emotions, and clarity. The candle's burning also sends energy out into the world in messages or requests from us to the Earth. Candles access unseen energy from the Earth and harness it to act as a guide.

Most candle magic is either personal or petition. A personal spell is where you are sending the energy into the universe to achieve your intention. This is where your intent is the main factor in which your magic will or will not work. It takes focus and a clear mind, but you will start seeing the change with more practice. A petition spell is where you ask a deity, ancestor, or specific god for help. Who you ask is up to you, but there is a lot of information on the different types of gods and deities. You can also request an element for help in candle magic. These spells are good as your magical energy is not drained; however, this might not always work.

You can infuse blood drops with oil to dress and charge your candle. The initial factor to ask yourself in candle magic is to attract or get rid of something. Becoming clear about what you're trying to accomplish will make the rest of this process much more workable. If you're manifesting, anoint your candle from top to bottom. If you're banishing, you will anoint from the bottom to the top. When making candles, you can add your blood to wax as well. The only thing is these candles will be for your work only—no one else's.

Save Me From Poverty

This is perfect to bring a small amount of money quickly to you.

ITEMS NEEDED:

- 1/4 teaspoon Ground Ginger
- 1/4 teaspoon Black Tea
- 4 drops Peppermint Oil

Green Seven-Day Candle
3 Drops Blood
Paper
Pen

DIRECTIONS:

Stick three holes in the top of the candle. Add 4 drops of oil to one hole. Add each herb to the remaining two. Write the amount of money needed on your piece of paper. Sign your name to it three times, adding a drop of your blood each time you sign.

Say nine times over the candle:

Money flows as my prosperity grows.

Light the candle and burn daily, repeating this mantra over the candle when you light it.

Butter Candle Spell

To bring quick cash in an emergency.

ITEMS NEEDED:

Bay Leaves
Yellow Flower Petals
Brown Sugar
Butter
4 drops Blood
Small Yellow Candle

DIRECTIONS:

Perform this spell before going to bed. Using the butter, dress the candle the same way as if it was oil while adding the four drops of blood.

Roll candle in brown sugar. Place yellow flower petals and bay leaves around the candle. Say over the candle:

Go straight to be once the candle has burned down.

Money should come to you in less than a week.

Protection Candle Spell

Prevent harm and misfortune by protecting yourself. With this basic protection spell.

ITEMS NEEDED:

1/2 teaspoon Mugwort
1/2 teaspoon Rosemary
1/2 teaspoon Sandalwood
1 Black Candle
4 drops Blood
Preferred Anointing Oil

DIRECTIONS:

Thoroughly mix dry ingredients. Combine a few drops of your blood with oil, and anoint the candle thoroughly in the mixture. Roll the candle in the dry mix. Light the candle, letting it burn all the way down. While the wax burns, along with your blood, oil, and herbs, you'll build powerful protective energy.

Reunite Lovers Candle Spell

This spell can be used when you are apart from your partner.

ITEMS NEEDED:

2 Red Candles (you can use human figure candles)

Rose Oil
3 drops Blood
Charger Plate

DIRECTIONS:

Anoint both candles with oil and blood and place them side-by-side on a charger plate or dish.

Light both candles thinking about your loved one as the wax starts to run together between the candles. Focus on your spell until the candles are joined by melted wax. Repeat the chant:

"Return to the place one came from
As our candles burn and wax run,
Soon, very soon
You and I again will be one."

Repeat several times until you feel the energy. Allow the candles to continue to burn until they go out on their own.

Abundance Candle Spell

The energy of the flame will help attract new financial possibilities to you.

ITEMS NEEDED:

1 Coin with Large Denomination
Cinnamon Oil
Vanilla Extract
3 drops Blood
Pin or Nail
1 Green Candle
Candle Holder

. . .

DIRECTIONS:

Use the pin or nail to carve the word ***Wealth*** along the candle side and then anoint the word with your blood, cinnamon, and vanilla. Set the coin in the bottom of your candle holder, set the candle over the top. Light the candle allowing it to burn down completely.

When the candle is done, leave the wax-covered coin in a safe place to help bring money into your life.

Two Become One Love Spell

This is a simple love spell that you can try as you are first getting into magic.

ITEMS NEEDED:

1 Red Candle
1 White Candle
2-3 drops Blood (or Blood Flakes)
Piece of Paper
Pen

DIRECTIONS:

Light each candle on your table or altar where they won't be interrupted. On the paper, write the traits you are seeking in a partner. Be practical and keep the list at no more than 6 points.

Split the paper in half, and burn one half in the flame of the red candle and the other half in the flame of the white candle. An ideal partner should come into your life shortly.

Bring Financial Possibilities to Me

Used to open avenues of prosperity to you.

ITEMS NEEDED:

1 Gold Candle
Your Personal Scented Oil
Clear Quartz Crystal
2-3 drops Blood (Or Blood Flakes)
Pen
Paper

DIRECTIONS:

Thursday during the new moon, charge your gold candle with your personal oil. Put the gold candle at the Northern end of your altar.

On the piece of paper, write:

"I welcome all possibilities for growing my financial foundation."

Set the paper in front of your candle and put the quartz crystal on top of the paper.

Light the candle and visualize a new financial opportunity moving into your life. Read aloud what you have written down on the paper. Burn the paper to release the desire. Allow the candle to burn down and discard the remains. Remember to give thanks for the prosperity you already have.

TWELVE

Talismans, Amulets, and Charm Bags

ADD YOUR BLOOD TO PETITION SPELL PAPERS. BLOOD CAN BE applied to sigils to strengthen their ability. Conjure Mojo Bags, Gris-Gris Bag, Spell Bag, etc., can have an included a drop of blood for added strength.

Working a spell where you burn the paper? Simply add a few drops of your blood onto the paper, after which you would burn it. This will free a portion of you into the divine level that we cannot see. Here's the thing, this where magic is accomplished. Offering a few drops of blood onto the soil outside will give in some measure part of you into Earth's energy. In turn, giving you more accessible power to using Earth magic.

If you've had some healing magic to perform, creating a talisman, amulet, or charm bag is an excellent idea. You can anoint a magic talisman or amulet with a couple of drops of your blood. Once it's dried, carry it in your pocket or on a cord around your neck. If you're constructing a healing bag, once you've filled it with herbs, stones, and additional items, add a drop or two of your own blood, afterward, sew or seal it shut.

Home Protection Amulet

This is an easy form of Hoodoo magic you can perform to safeguard your home from negative energies.

ITEMS NEEDED:

9 White Mustard Seeds
Square Piece of Red Flannel Cloth
2-3 drops Blood (or Blood Flakes)
1 Metal Nail

DIRECTIONS:

Place blood in the center of the red cloth. Add and wrap the seeds in a bundle of red flannel, and nail the charm to the back of your front door. This will keep bad energy and negative spells out of your home.

Silver Dime Protection Spell

I love this spell. Most people have trouble finding a silver dime.

ITEMS NEEDED:

3 inch Square Paper
King Solomon Oil
Fifth Pentacle Of Saturn
Sator Square
Pen
Silver Dime (1964 or earlier)
Red Pepper Seeds
Grains Of Paradise
4 drops Blood

. . .

DIRECTIONS:

On one side of the paper, write a Sator square.

S A T O R
A R E P O
T E N E T
O P E R A
R O T A S

On the other side, draw the Fifth Pentacle of Saturn.

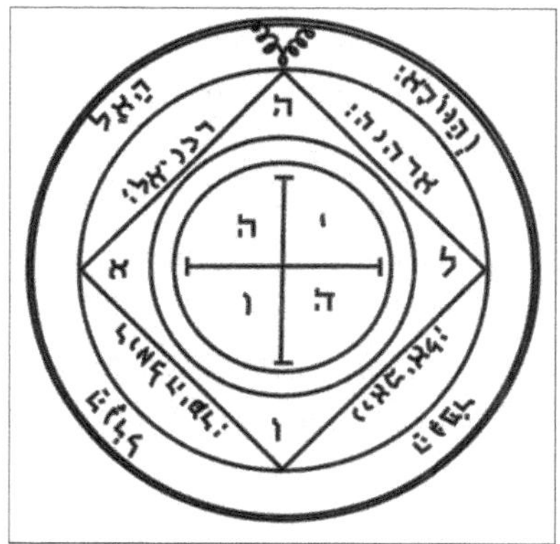

Add a drop of blood to each corner, followed by dressing the paper's edge with King Solomon oil. Fold opposite corners up, create a pocket and place the dime inside and Grains of Paradise and Red Pepper seeds. Fold the two sides in together, followed by the top to close your packet. Hide this under your doorstep or somewhere near your front door.

Creating a Honey Jar

Bees have been associate with intelligence and serve as messengers within this realm and the spirit world. Their honey has been used in folklore to treat every ailment under the sun and be used for its magical properties.

ITEMS NEEDED

Honey
Small Jar
Blood (Menstrual or not)or Dried Blood Flakes
Paper
Pen

DIRECTIONS:

Add honey and a drop or two of your menstrual blood (or flakes) to a jar. Take your piece of paper and draw a flower with petals. In its center, write a word to signify your intent. This is the energy or goal you wish to attract into your life.

Write a word or phrase in each of the flower's petals that relates to that goal. If origami is your forte, you can shape a flower from the paper.

Seal your honey jar and set it somewhere you can see it every day. Apply it as an element of your rituals if you like. Open your jar every month to add a fresh drop or two of your menstrual blood to add energy to the honey jar's collective magic.

THIRTEEN

Creating Your Magical Ink

THE MOST INFLUENTIAL TYPE OF MAGICAL INKS IS BLOOD INKS. Blood inks are excellent, and every witch should have one for specific intentions.

Blood inks have the power to direct your intentions and work with whatever your heart seeks. Using the appropriate magic ink for the right purpose will provide energy to your spells and magical workings.

Whether you make your own magical ink or not, having it in your arsenal will definitely take your magic to the next level!

Suppose you are the Witch who chooses to instill their magical tools with their essence. Why not create a collection of beautiful inks to include in your tool selection. Writing is magic. Sigils and symbols are magic. Menstrual blood is a powerful ink to be used in any manner.

Making your own ink for your Book of Shadows, dream journals, etc., will increase the energy you instill into the pages and bring about your work.

Dragon's Blood Ink

Dragon's blood is used to enhance the energy of spells and any spells involving faith, protection, authority, and influence. Another plus part is that it can also be used to reinforce potions and mixtures.

Mix it with any incense or herbal mixture to raise the potion's capability.

ITEMS NEEDED:

1/2 teaspoon part dragon's blood
1 ounces alcohol
1/2 teaspoon part Arabic Gum
2 -3 drops of blood or blood flakes

DIRECTIONS:

Mix the ingredients one at a time, adding the Arabic Gum last. A little at a time until you reach the thickness you want. Filter through a cloth and store in a dark bottle. Most important thing: Label!

Dove's Blood Ink

Dove's blood ink is best applied for writing out the most lively and best-intentioned spells and for utilization in productivity, love spells, fertility, and wealth rituals. Dove's blood ink can likewise be used to establish an agreement or a commitment and inscribe on amulets and talismans.

ITEMS NEEDED:

3 teaspoon Part Dragon's Blood
3 teaspoon Gum Arabic Powder

1 ounce Alcohol
6 drops Cinnamon Oil
6 drops Bay Oil
6 drops Rose Oil
3 drops Blood or Blood Flakes

DIRECTIONS:

Combine the ingredients adding the Arabic powder last, a little at a time, until you reach the consistency you want. If at any time you find your ink too thick, slowly add alcohol to thin it out. If it's too thin, slowly add Arabic Gum powder, to thicken it up.

Butterfly Ink

Butterfly ink a genuinely powerful tool every Witch should have. Whether urban, rural, secluded, shaman, bruja, pagan, natural-born, and more. Butterfly Ink is for preparing talismans, prayers, and invocations, corresponding with the Element of the Air.

ITEMS NEEDED:

2 teaspoon Saffron Powder
3 teaspoon Arabic Gum Powder
1 ounce Alcohol
3 drops Blood or Blood Flakes
Heat Resistance Container
Small Pot

DIRECTIONS:

Placing saffron powder into a heat resistance container, boil the alcohol. Pour alcohol over the saffron. Adding blood, stir clockwise and slowly add the Arabic gum. If at any time you find your ink too thick, slowly add alcohol to thin it out. If it's too thin, slowly add Arabic Gum powder, to thicken it up. Put the mixture in the refrigerator for 3 hours to cool and pour into a dark-colored bottle. Remember to label.

Bat's Blood Magical Ink

Bat's blood ink is one magical ink you should use cautiously. Bat's blood ink should be used to write spells of misfortune, havoc, and putting hexes. Removing obstacles caused by black magic, curses, etc., and thus, turning bad luck into good. But you can also use bat's blood ink to protect yourself from hexes. As well as to undo jinxes done to you.

ITEMS NEEDED:

1 teaspoon Dragon's Blood Resin Powder
1 teaspoon Myrrh Resin Powder
3 teaspoon Arabic Gum Powder
½ ounce Alcohol
½ cup Water
3 drops Blood or Blood Flakes
Red Food Coloring
Small Pot

DIRECTIONS:

Boil water. Lower the temperature and slowly pour the Arabic Gum powder. Stir until it is fully absorbed. Next, add in Dragon's Blood resin powder, Myrrh resin powder, and your blood. Keep stirring until you have a honey-like consistency.. remove from heat and put the mixture in the refrigerator for 2 hours to cool. Add the alcohol and food coloring. Stir until you reach the correct thickness.

If at any time you find your ink too thick, slowly add alcohol to thin it out. If it's too thin, slowly add Arabic Gum powder to thicken it up. Pour into a dark-colored bottle. Remember to label.

Adding a few drops of Uncrossing or Banishing oil to your Bat's Blood ink creates the perfect empowered ink. Use it to write on paper obstacles or problems you may be having. Remember, this for issues you may be having trouble with. Not people.

Throw the papers into a fire and let them burn to ashes. Always concentrated on whatever you are doing while using Bat's Blood Ink.

If at any time you find your ink too thick, slowly add alcohol to thin it out. If it's too thin, slowly add Arabic Gum powder to thicken it up.

FOURTEEN

Petitions and Sigils

NOW THAT YOU HAVE THE INK, HERE ARE A FEW PETITION papers you a try your hand at.

In some magical practices, petitions or requests are created on paper and delivered to the spirits or the gods. If you wish to bring prosperity, or abundance protection, love, etc., your way, write a petition to the spirits, ancestors, or spirits of your practice.

Once you have your paper composed, you can fix and dress it with relevant oils to your spell, sprinkle herbs or powders in it, and place any small amount of tag lock or personal items, including blood, on top of the paper. Fold directed toward you as in bringing in graces, or away from you if you are getting rid of something. Turn and fold paper again in the direction you are engaged with. Turn a third time, repeating the previous step. Now completed, place the paper for where it was created for, whether a poppet, under a candle, mojo bag, etc. Some papers can be burned by the candle's fire to deliver the invocation into the universe.

There are many methods to write petitions papers, so get imaginative. in time you'll start using papers in your work. you will immediately discover new means to create them.

Once it's written down, sign it by putting a dot of blood on the paper with your fingertip. The petition can then be rolled up, set under a candle, or sent out to the universe in your belief structure's typical manner.

Find Me My Soul Mate

A very simple spell requiring a few items.

ITEMS NEEDED:

Paper
Pen
2-3 drops Blood

DIRECTIONS:

Focus on what you want in your soul mate. Have a list in your mind what traits your soul mate has.

Write in the present tense:

"I have met my soul mate
He or she is ______ (list the traits).
We are so happy together.
Every day."

Draw a pentacle on the top left corner of paper. Dab a drop of blood to the center of the pentacle. Fold the paper towards you, turn and fold again towards you. Make the packet as small as you can.

During a waxing moon, bury your packet in your yard. Your soul mate will soon seek you out.

Money Petition Paper

Simple money petition to attract money.

. . .

ITEMS NEEDED:

Paper
Pen
4 drops Blood

DIRECTIONS:

Write the amount you are requesting in a grid for. Turn your petition paper 90 degrees (a quarter turn) to the right.

$1000	$1000	$1000
$1000	$1000	$1000
$1000	$1000	$1000

Write *"Come to me,"* over the amount you are requesting.

Turn your petition paper 90 degrees again to the right to sign the petition.

Turn your petition paper 90 degrees to the right. Here you will write the amount you want and the date desired. You will write this, turn, write, turn, write, turn, and write, making sure the phrase overlaps the previous one. I've written, "$1,000 comes to me by January 1, 2021."

Dispel and Eliminate

This spell is if you would prefer not to be associated with a person in your life.

ITEMS NEEDED:

Black Construction Paper
Pen
4 drops Blood

DIRECTIONS:

Write the individual's name in the middle of the paper. It doesn't make a difference if you can't really read it. Add blood on top of the name you've written. Fold the paper away from you as small as possible. Take the package outside to bury it in the ground. Once it's covered, say:

"Into the ground
You won't be found
You're not around
I don't hear your sound."

Walk over the place you've buried the paper, and that individual will soon disappear from your life.

Quarrel No More

A spell to end the arguments in your home.

ITEMS NEEDED:

1 teaspoon Catnip
1 teaspoon Orris Root
1 teaspoon Lavender Flowers
½ cup Sugar
Small Bowl with Lid
2-3 drops Blood (Or Blood Flakes)
Paper
Pen

DIRECTIONS:

Write your spouse or lover's name and date of birth three times on the piece of paper. Place catnip, orris root, lavender flowers, and your blood in the middle of the paper covering their name. Fold corner to corner towards you, making a packet. Place in bowl and cover with sugar. Add lid.

Chant over daily nine times:

"(Name), be at peace. Love me. Don't fight me any longer."

Keep bowl at the back of the stove or somewhere warm.

Note: For men, use eve root instead of the orris root.

Creating and Charging Sigils

Blood is ideal for charging sigils. Menstrual blood even more so. Rubbing blood to a sigil inserts a piece of your life force into the image. The next time you create a sigil, empower it with your blood. The blood will trigger its powers faster.

What Is A Sigil?

A sigil is a two-dimensional design that has an incredibly magical effect.

A sigil can be compared to an encrypted message. It may seem like an abstract combination of squiggles, but it really represents a specific idea. The idea that a sigil is designed to represent is its magical purpose.

ITEMS NEEDED:

Pen or Pencil
Blank Paper
A Candle
2-3 drops Blood
Ceramic Bowl
Matches or Lighter

1. Write Down Your Intention

All magic starts with the purpose. Your intention is the most essential part of any magical working. Sigils are an excellent way to work at creating your intention.

MY BUSINESS GROWS

2. Remove Any Vowels and Repeats

Studying the intention, eliminate or cross out all of the

vowels and any repeating, leaving behind only one of each consonant from the initial sentence.

MYBSNSSGRWS

3. Streamline the Letters

You can divide or break down the letters into lines and curves or leave them as they are.

MYBSNGW

4. Arrange the Shapes

Work with these shapes to try to fit them into a single glyph. It'll take some rearranging and several efforts to create a powerful image. You can add or subtract from it. You see where I added a dot.

5. Activate the Sigil

In some occurrences, simply drawing it may be enough to activate the sigil. There are some occasions where they call for a bit more. Focus on what the sigil represents. Study at the symbol you've designed, and look back at the reason you chose it. Once done, include a dab of your blood.

6. Discharging the Sigil

There are several ways to discharge the emotional interest in the sigil. In this situation, you're only going to be burning the paper you've written it on. Lighting one side put it in the bowl. Making sure you don't burn yourself in the process.

As it burns, imagine all of the emotional investment you've placed in the sigil. Also, the idea it represents. It is being transformed into a new form made of the universal forces of light and heat. Visualize that light and energy expanding out from this minute. Picture the glow of the sigil's little light reaching across your entire life. Observe it until the flame goes out.

7. Let It Go

Once the burning of the sigil has gone out, the sigil is then considered discharged. The process of the sigil has begun, and it no longer requires your awareness. Let the sigil and what it means, go. It will perform the same, even if you never reflect on it repeatedly. That doesn't mean that you should evade the sigil or anything. It's simply done.

. . .

NOTE: Don't worry if the flame unexpectedly goes out through this process. It doesn't signify the sigil creation has failed. Just reignite the residual paper. This step's power comes from the intention to release the sigil's exertion, not if the paper needs to be relit.

FIFTEEN

Bonus Recipes

Come To Me Oil

Come to me Oil is an excellent favorite for anointing love spell candles and figure candles. Choose one candle to represent yourself and your intended partner. Dress them with your oil and burn them together.

ITEMS NEEDED:

1 drop Rose
1 drop Jasmine
1 drop Gardenia
1 drop Lemon Oil
2-3 drops Blood (or Blood Flakes)
1 ounce Olive Oil

DIRECTIONS:

Add together, keep in a dark bottle and use to anoint candles on love spells.

Come to Me Incense

Items Needed:

1/2 Cup Shredded Candle Wax
1 tablespoon Potato Starch, Cornstarch, or Tapioca Flour
1 Long Stem Rose
Extra Rose Petals
1 handful Dried Lavender or Jasmine
1 teaspoon Coriander
1/4 teaspoon Black Coffee Powder
1 spoonful Raw Sugar
2-3 drops Blood (or Blood Flakes)

DIRECTIONS:

Mix all of these ingredients thoroughly. Place in a small square pan and melt slowly. Allow this to cool, and then you can break off small portions as required.

Burn on charcoal, open a window enabling some of the smoke to get outside, and travel to your desired one.

Attraction Oil

Items Needed:

1 teaspoon Lovage Herb
1 teaspoon Lemon Peel
1 teaspoon Rose Petals
1/2 teaspoon Lemon Balm
2-3 drops Blood (or Blood Flakes)
1 ounce Sweet Almond Oil
Small piece Lodestone

DIRECTIONS:

Mix herbs in oil. 3 days before the full moon, place under a waxing moon until the moon is full. Place 3 drops of oil on a cotton ball and put it in your shoes for luck in love. To draw new love, anoint your forehead, below your heart, and above your naval.

Conclusion

Blood spells cannot be reversed. Your blood is your spirit. Without your blood, a spell carries your intention, direction, and focus. With your blood, a spell draws all this, together with a piece of you. Blood spells call for somewhat a bit more strength than non-blood spells. The DNA in your blood pulsates at the identical rhythm as the blood in your body. Even after it has dried out, the DNA in the blood is nonetheless you. You are connected to the spell just as you would be connected to a magical item. Breaking a blood spell is practically unthinkable. A blood spell effects are more potent than ordinary magic, for all those concerned, for better or worse.

Like any other type of magic, blood magic spells and rituals can either be used for good or evil. Because of this, make every effort to be the person who practices magic to make things better, not worse. Always remember that karmic energy is impacted by everything you do. This means like attract like. If you work at doing good, it will come your way.

As a final point, practicing regularly is what will make you better. Everyone starts at square one. Build yourself up to casting the more significant blood magic spells. So, if you ever notice yourself in doubt, all you need to do is going back to the basics.

References

aminoapps.com/c/pagans-witches/page/blog/blood-magic/moP7_DZ8Hku0LDEPW6EdadqRoemreQQ23Rd

Baker, Aryn. "Affirming a Faith Bathed in Blood." Time. Time Inc. January 2007.

blackwitchcoven.com/beginners-blood-magick-dos-donts

Blood sacrifice and modern Paganisms | Paganism. https://wildhunt.org/2014/04/perspectives-blood-sacrifice.html

Copeman, Jacob. "Blood will have Blood: A Study in Indian Political Ritual." Social Analysis 48 (2004): 126-48. EBSCO HOST. Web. 7 November 2011.

crescentcityconjure.us/

exemplore.com/wicca-witchcraft/Witchcraft-for-Beginners-What-You-Should-Know-about-Blood-Magic

face2faceafrica.com/article/uncovering-the-disgusting-ritual-of-using-menstrual-blood-to-keep-lovers-at-bay

groveandgrotto.com/blogs/articles/how-to-cleanse-and-charge-a-new-amulet-or-talisman

occult-world.com/blood-demonology

pandagossips.com

Ritual Use of Blood, Yesterday and Today – Llewellyn

Unbound. https://www.llewellyn.com/blog/2015/08/ritual-use-of-blood-yesterday-and-today/

wildhunt.org/2014/04/perspectives-blood-sacrifice.html

witchofapollo.tumblr.com/post/186667158321/blood-magick-101-one-of-the-most-common-things-i

www.britannica.com/topic/sacrifice-religion/Blood-offerings

www.learnreligions.com/blood-magic-4777683

www.patheos.com/blogs/witchofthewoodwithraven-wood/2017/12/lets-play-in-the-dark-shall-we-blood-magick/

www.quailbellmagazine.com/

www.waningmoon.com/darkpagan/lib/lib0003.shtml

About the Author

Monique Joiner Siedlak is a writer, witch, and warrior on a mission to awaken people to their greatest potential through the power of storytelling infused with mysticism, modern paganism, and new age spirituality. At the young age of 12, she began rigorously studying the fascinating philosophy of Wicca. By the time she was 20, she was self-initiated into the craft, and hasn't looked back ever since. To this day, she has authored over 40 books pertaining to the magick and mysteries of life.

To find out more about Monique Joiner Siedlak artistically, spiritually, and personally, feel free to visit her **official website**.

www.mojosiedlak.com

facebook.com/mojosiedlak
twitter.com/mojosiedlak
instagram.com/mojosiedlak
pinterest.com/mojosiedlak
bookbub.com/authors/monique-joiner-siedlak

Other Books by Monique

Practical Magick

Wiccan Basics

Candle Magick

Wiccan Spells

Love Spells

Abundance Spells

Herb Magick

Moon Magick

Creating Your Own Spells

Gypsy Magic

Protection Magick

Celtic Magick

Personal and Self Development

Creative Visualization

Astral Projection for Beginners

Meditation for Beginners

Reiki for Beginners

Manifesting With the Law of Attraction

Stress Management

Being an Empath Today

Get a Handle on Life

Get a Handle on Anxiety

Get a Handle on Depression

Get a Handle on Procrastination

The Yoga Collective

Yoga for Beginners

Yoga for Stress

Yoga for Back Pain

Yoga for Weight Loss

Yoga for Flexibility

Yoga for Advanced Beginners

Yoga for Fitness

Yoga for Runners

Yoga for Energy

Yoga for Your Sex Life

Yoga To Beat Depression and Anxiety

Yoga for Menstruation

Yoga to Detox Your Body

Yoga to Tone Your Body

A Natural Beautiful You

Creating Your Own Body Butter

Creating Your Own Body Scrub

Creating Your Own Body Spray

Other Books by Monique

Practical Magick

Wiccan Basics

Candle Magick

Wiccan Spells

Love Spells

Abundance Spells

Herb Magick

Moon Magick

Creating Your Own Spells

Gypsy Magic

Protection Magick

Celtic Magick

Personal and Self Development

Creative Visualization

Astral Projection for Beginners

Meditation for Beginners

Reiki for Beginners

Manifesting With the Law of Attraction

Stress Management

Being an Empath Today

Get a Handle on Life

Get a Handle on Anxiety

Get a Handle on Depression

Get a Handle on Procrastination

The Yoga Collective

Yoga for Beginners

Yoga for Stress

Yoga for Back Pain

Yoga for Weight Loss

Yoga for Flexibility

Yoga for Advanced Beginners

Yoga for Fitness

Yoga for Runners

Yoga for Energy

Yoga for Your Sex Life

Yoga To Beat Depression and Anxiety

Yoga for Menstruation

Yoga to Detox Your Body

Yoga to Tone Your Body

A Natural Beautiful You

Creating Your Own Body Butter

Creating Your Own Body Scrub

Creating Your Own Body Spray

WANT UPDATES,
FREEBIES & GIVEAWAYS?!
MONIQUE JOINER SIEDLAK
THE
ORISHAS
JOIN MY
NEWSLETTER!
mojosiedlak.com/newsletter-signup

THANK YOU FOR READING MY BOOK! I REALLY APPRECIATE ALL OF YOUR FEEDBACK AND I LOVE TO HEAR WHAT YOU HAVE TO SAY. PLEASE LEAVE YOUR REVIEW AT YOUR FAVORITE RETAILER!

www.ingramcontent.com/pod-product-compliance
Lightning Source LLC
LaVergne TN
LVHW010107110826
845155LV00028B/522

* 9 7 8 1 9 5 0 3 7 8 5 9 3 *